GORGEOUSLY GRUESOME
ZOMBIES

GORGEOUSLY GRUESOME
ZOMBIES

Raise your very own undead zombie army

Bath · New York · Singapore · Hong Kong · Cologne · Delhi
Melbourne · Amsterdam · Johannesburg · Auckland · Shenzhen

First published by Parragon in 2012

Parragon
Queen Street House
4 Queen Street
Bath BA1 1HE, UK
www.parragon.com

Copyright © Parragon Books Ltd 2012
Designed by Pink Creative
Illustrations by Ummagumma
Project managed by Frances Prior-Reeves

ISBN 978-1-4454-8864-6

Printed in China

GORGEOUSLY GRUESOME
ZOMBIES

The zombies are here and set to take over the world – they just need you to sew on their missing limbs, stuff their brains back in their heads and create a unique zombie army. Don't let looks mislead you – there's nothing cute about these zombies. They'll eat their way through everything in their path before you can even think about trying to stop them.

Create all of these characters if you dare but remember about the power of numbers – maybe some would be best as flesh-eating gifts for your friends. All you need to raise each zombie from the dead is listed at the start of the instructions. For all projects you'll need a pair of scissors and a needle. You might also find pins helpful to attach your paper template to the fabric before cutting. All the templates you need are included in the back, ready for you to copy them, cut them out and start creating your own zombie army.

If you want to start with an easier project try Mobile Zomphone (p.28) and then move on to the complex zombie intricacies of Octozombie (p.8). Zombies are being found anywhere and everywhere, in schools, in your salad and even pinned to your shirt – it's an epidemic. Be careful they don't overpower you!

MATERIALS

Blue felt, pink felt, turquoise felt, brown felt, red felt, grey felt, white felt
Red, dark blue and black embroidery thread
2cm (¾ inch) of black hook and loop fabric
Hole punch, 2 small white beads
Toy stuffing, Pins, Craft glue
Embroidery Needle, Scissors
Templates from page 40

MAKING `OCTOZOMBIE`

1 Photocopy or trace all the templates on page 40. Cut the BODY from blue felt, then sew a line of dripping blood, using red thread along the bite mark.

2 Cut the BRAIN from pink felt and glue to the back of the BODY so it shows behind the bite mark. Now sew a line of 'stitching' using black thread.

OCTOZOMBIE

If you thought you were safe on dry land, you were wrong. With eight legs of terrifying zombie, he's quicker than you'd expect.

3 Cut LEGS 1,2,3,4 and LEG 8 from turquoise felt. Cut the BODY BACK from blue felt. Glue the legs in position onto the BODY BACK.

4 Sew the BODY to the BODY BACK with dark blue thread, sandwiching the top ends of the legs. Leave the BRAIN area open and fill the body with stuffing.

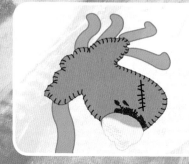

5 Close the opening by gluing the exposed BRAIN to the BODY BACK.

6 Cut LEGS 5,6,7 from turquoise felt and LEGS 5,6,7 BACK from blue felt. Glue them together.

7 Cut a circle about 1cm (½ inch) diameter from the hook and loop fabric. Sew the hook side of the fabric to the turquoise side of LEGS 5,6,7 with dark blue thread.

8 Sew an area of dripping blood around the hook and loop fabric.

9 Cut 14 SUCKERS from brown felt and glue to the turquoise side of the LEGS 5,6,7. These can be cut either by hand or by using a hole punch.

10 Turn the body over and sew the loop circle to the BODY BACK with dark blue thread at the position shown.

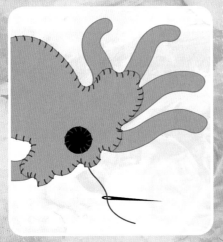

12 Cut the two EYES from red felt. Now sew a white bead to each of the EYES using black thread. Glue the EYES to the BODY.

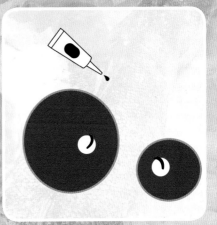

11 Turn the Octozombie back over the correct way. Cut 16 SUCKERS from brown felt and glue onto the legs.

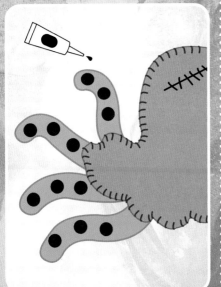

13 Cut the MOUTH from grey felt and the TEETH from white felt. Glue the TEETH in place on the MOUTH, then glue to the BODY.

ZOMBILLAR

This zombie will hide among your salad leaves and you won't see him until it's too late. First he will eat your plants, then you!

MAKING `ZOMBILLAR`

1 Photocopy or trace all the templates on page 41. Cut the BODY LEFT PANEL from dark green felt and the BODY MIDDLE PANEL from light green felt. Glue the two together as shown.

2 Cut the BODY RIGHT PANEL from dark green felt. Glue the BODY RIGHT PANEL to the end of the BODY MIDDLE PANEL.

MATERIALS

Dark green felt, light green felt, grey felt, yellow felt, black felt

Light green, red, light blue, white and grey embroidery thread

2 small red beads, 3 white bead tubes

Toy stuffing

Pins, Craft glue, Embroidery needle

Scissors

Templates from page 41

3 Cut the BODY BACK from dark green felt and then sew the three body panels to the BODY BACK with light green thread, leaving the bite mark as an opening and fill with stuffing.

EAT YOUR GREENS!

4 Sew up the opening with red thread to create a dripping blood effect.

5 Using six-strand light blue thread, sew on the hair to the top edge of the body. Do this by pushing the needle through the felt and then tying a knot. Trim the thread to about 2cm (¾ inch) long and then tease out the strands of thread.

6 Cut the two EYES from black felt. Using six-strand red thread, tie a knot in one end of the thread. Now thread on a red bead, pushing it up to the knot. Now stitch to the EYE leaving about 1cm (½ inch) length of thread so the bead dangles down. Repeat for the second eye.

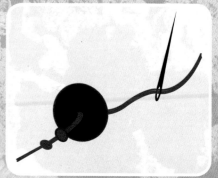

7 Cut the MOUTH from black felt. Now sew the three bead tubes to the mouth with white thread to create the teeth.

8 Cut the two HEAD panels from grey felt. Glue the EYES and MOUTH to one of the FACE panels.

9 Now sew the two HEAD panels together with grey thread, leaving a small opening and fill with stuffing. Then close up the opening.

10 Turn the body over and sew to the HEAD with light green thread.

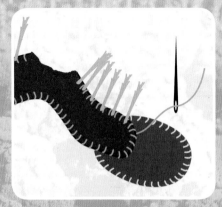

11 Cut the two TENTACLES and ten FEET from yellow felt. Glue the small ends of the TENTACLES to the top edge of the HEAD. Glue the FEET to the bottom edge of the BODY.

MATERIALS

White felt, beige felt, black felt, red felt, orange felt

White, black and red embroidery thread

2 small red beads

Toy stuffing

Pins, Craft glue

Embroidery needle

Scissors

Templates from page 42

MAKING `ZOMBIE TRAFFIC CONE`

1 Photocopy or trace all the templates on page 42. Cut the CONE BAND from white felt and the TEETH from beige felt. Slide the TEETH through the slit in the CONE BAND and glue in place.

2 Cut the two EYES from black felt. Take a length of six-strand white thread and tie a knot in one end. Now thread a bead over the thread and push it down to the knot. Sew the thread through the centre of one of the EYES, leaving about 1cm (½ inch) of thread to allow the bead to dangle down. Repeat for the second eye and then glue them to the CONE BAND, just above the mouth.

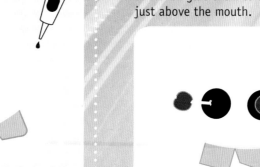

ZOMBIE TRAFFIC CONE

Causing more accidents than they prevent, the Zombie Traffic Cones are taking over the world. Don't trust their directions.

3 Cut BLOOD 1 and BLOOD 2 from red felt and glue them together.

4 Cut the CONE FRONT from orange felt, remembering to cut the slit, too. Now slide the BLOOD into the slit and glue in place.

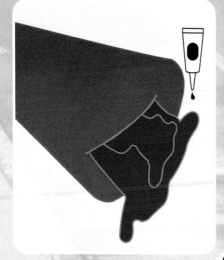

5 Cut the BASE from black felt and glue behind the CONE FRONT.

6 Glue the CONE BAND in position.

TRAFFIC CHAOS!

7 Sew the line of 'stitching' across the top of the cone, using black thread.

8 Sew the second line of 'stitching' across the bottom half of the cone in black thread.

9 Using red thread, sew the top bite area of the cone to create dripping blood.

10 Cut the CONE BACK from orange felt and sew to the back of the cone, leaving a small opening.

11 Fill the cone with a small amount of stuffing and then close up the opening.

SCHOOLBOY ZOMBIE

Don't let looks mislead you – there's nothing cute about this picture-perfect schoolboy. He'll eat his way out of detention before you can even think to expel him.

MAKING `SCHOOLBOY ZOMBIE`

1 Photocopy or trace all the templates on page 43. Cut the SHIRT from white felt, the SHORTS from red felt and the LEGS from grey felt. Glue the LEGS to the bottom of the SHORTS and then the SHORTS to the bottom edge of the SHIRT.

2 Cut the ARMS from grey felt and glue them to the sleeves in the SHIRT. Cut the TIE from red felt and the two COLLARS from white felt. Glue the TIE to the 'V' of the SHIRT and the COLLARS to either side of the TIE. Cut the CHEST from grey felt and glue behind the neck of the shirt.

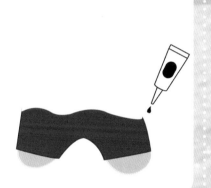

MATERIALS

White felt, red felt, grey felt, brown felt

Black and red embroidery thread

1 button, 1 bead

Toy stuffing

Pins

Craft glue

Embroidery needle

Scissors

Templates from page 43

3 Cut the BODY BACK from grey felt and lay the body on top of the BODY BACK. Sew the bite mark with red thread to create some blood.

6 Sew the two HEAD panels together with black thread, leaving a small opening. Fill the HEAD with a small amount of stuffing and then close up the opening.

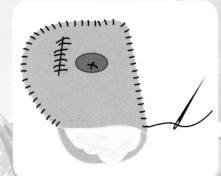

4 Now sew the rest of the body together with black thread, leaving a small opening and fill with stuffing. Close up the opening.

DETENTION!

5 Cut the two HEAD panels from grey felt. Take one of the HEAD panels and, with black thread, sew a 'stitch' mouth. Then sew the button just above the mouth with black thread.

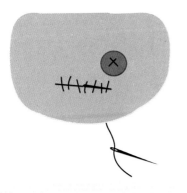

7 Turn the body over and sew to the HEAD with black thread.

8 Cut the SATCHEL and FLAP from brown felt. Glue the FLAP to the top edge of the SATCHEL. Finish by sewing a couple of stitches, with black thread, to create the buckles on the straps.

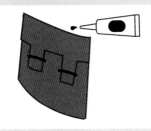

9 Cut the STRAP from brown felt and glue across the body. Then glue the SATCHEL to the end of the STRAP on one side of the body.

10 Cut the EYE from brown felt. Take a length of six-strand red thread and tie a knot in one end. Feed on the bead. Now stitch the other end of the thread to the centre of the EYE, leaving about 1cm (½ inch) of thread so the bead dangles down. Cut any excess thread from the end of the bead.

11 Glue the EYE to the HEAD. Cut the CAP and CAP PEAK from red felt. Glue the PEAK behind the CAP and then glue the whole CAP to the side of the HEAD.

MATERIALS

Dark blue felt, light blue felt, beige felt, turquoise felt, red felt, white felt

Pink, red and black embroidery thread

1 small white button with 4 holes

1 medium-sized safety pin

Toy stuffing

Pins, Craft glue

Embroidery needle

Scissors

Templates from page 44

MAKING `ZOMBIE PIN BADGE`

1 Photocopy or trace all the templates on page 44. Cut the BADGE FRONT from dark blue felt and the CROSS from light blue felt. Glue the CROSS to the BADGE FRONT.

2 Cut the BADGE BACK from turquoise felt and the ARM from beige felt. Glue the ARM in place as shown.

ZOMBIE PIN BADGE

Wear this gruesome badge with pride and show you're a zombie supporter – they're just misunderstood ... aren't they? Dare you pin it to your shirt?

5 Now place the BADGE FRONT on top of the BADGE BACK and stitch in place with pink thread. Leave the bite area open.

3 Cut the HEART from red felt. Using pink thread, sew a few lines to the HEART to define some shape.

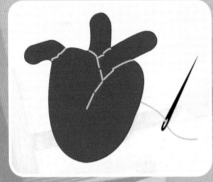

6 Stuff the BADGE with a small amount of stuffing.

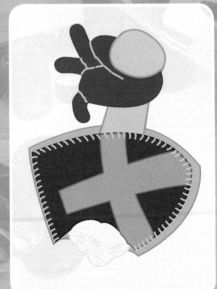

4 Glue the HEART towards the end of the ARM. Now cut the HAND from beige felt and glue in place, covering some of the HEART.

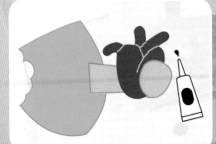

7 Close up the opening by stitching a line of blood with red thread.

SUPPORT
THE CAUSE!

8 Cut the BLOOD from red felt and glue in place. Now use black thread to create the 'stitched' mouth, staying close to the top edge of the BLOOD.

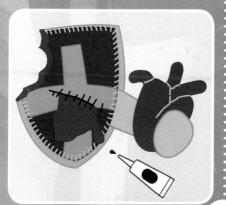

9 Cut the EYE SOCKETS from beige felt. Cut the EYE from white felt. Sew the EYE to the larger EYE SOCKET with black thread in a cross shape. Now sew the button to the smaller EYE SOCKET with black thread, allowing enough thread so that the button dangles. Glue the EYE SOCKET in place onto the BADGE FRONT.

10 Turn the badge over and with red thread, sew the safety pin in place. Be careful not to stab yourself!

MOBILE ZOMPHONE

If you wanted to phone someone to warn them of the zombie apocalypse, you might want to find a payphone. This one'll have your ear off!

MAKING `MOBILE ZOMPHONE`

1 Photocopy or trace all the templates on page 45. Cut the SCREEN from beige felt, remembering to cut out the mouth area. Cut the TEETH from white felt and glue to the back of the mouth area.

2 Cut the MOUTH from dark red felt and glue to the back of the SCREEN and TEETH.

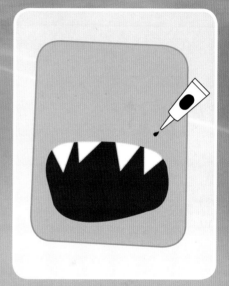

MATERIALS

Beige felt, white felt, dark red felt, black felt, red felt, grey felt, green felt, blue felt

Grey, white and black embroidery thread

Toy stuffing

Pins

Craft glue

Embroidery needle

Scissors

Templates from page 45

3 Cut the two PHONE panels from black felt. Now place the screen onto one of the PHONE panels so that it sits with more space at the bottom than the top. Stitch around the outside of the screen in grey thread.

4 Cut the MICROPHONE and SPEAKER from grey felt. Stitch them in place with grey thread.

5 Cut the two BUTTONS: one from green felt and the other from red felt. Take the red BUTTON and using white thread, stitch the outline of a telephone receiver in the down position.

6 Now take the green BUTTON and stitch, with white thread, a telephone receiver in the up position.

7 Glue the two BUTTONS either side of the MICROPHONE.

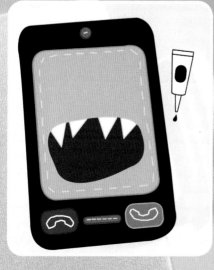

9 Cut the BLOOD from the red felt and glue in position on the MOUTH.

8 Cut the two EYES from blue felt and stitch a cross on each one, using black thread.

10 Take the remaining PHONE panel and stitch it to the back of the other PHONE panel, with grey thread. Leave a small opening and fill the phone with stuffing. Not too much, just enough to give it shape. Then close up the opening.

MATERIALS

Dark brown felt, dark green felt, magenta felt, mid-green felt, light green felt, light brown felt, white felt
Light blue, pink, black, red and grey embroidery thread
1 small black bead
Toy stuffing, Pins, Craft glue
Embroidery needle
Scissors
Templates from page 46

MAKING `VENUS FLYTRAP ZOMBIE`

1 Photocopy or trace all the templates on page 46. Cut the POT FRONT from dark brown felt and the STEM from dark green felt. Glue the stem to the top part of the POT FRONT.

2 Cut the MOUTH from magenta felt and the LEAF from mid-green felt. Glue the MOUTH and LEAF in the positions shown.

VENUS FLYTRAP ZOMBIE

A fly is just an appetizer for this zombie. He'll have your finger, and maybe more, for its main course. Brain palate cleanser anyone?

3 Cut the MOUTH TOP and MOUTH BOTTOM from light green felt. Glue them to the top and bottom areas of the MOUTH.

5 Now continue to sew up the rest of the plant, leaving a small opening. Fill with stuffing and close up the opening.

4 Cut the BACK from dark green felt and lay behind the plant parts you've just made. Now sew the BACK to the front with light blue thread, starting with the head of the plant. Before sewing too much, stuff the head with a small amount of stuffing.

6 Using pink thread, sew a line of stitching across the centre of the mouth, going right through both thicknesses of felt to create a pinched cushion effect.

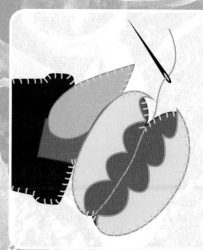

7 Cut the POT RIM from light brown felt and glue in place, covering the bottom edge of the STEM.

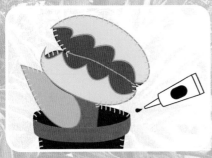

8 Using grey thread, sew a line of 'stitching' across the pot.

9 Cut the EYES from white felt. Using black thread, sew a cross on the right EYE. Now take a length of six-strand red thread and tie a knot in one end. Feed on the bead and push it down to the knot. Now sew the thread to the right EYE leaving about 1cm (½ inch) of thread to enable the bead to dangle. Trim off any excess thread from the bead end.

10 Glue the EYES to the top edge of the head.

VOODOO ZOMBIE

You can stick as many pins in him as you like, but he just won't die!

MATERIALS

Red felt, black felt

White and red embroidery thread

5 sewing pins with white plastic heads

1 small white button

Toy stuffing

Pins, Craft glue

Embroidery needle

Scissors

Templates from page 47

MAKING `VOODOO ZOMBIE`

1 Photocopy or trace all the templates on page 47. Cut the BODY from black felt. Using white thread, sew the 'stitching' lines across the arms, legs and up the stomach.

2 Cut the BODY BACK from black felt and then sew to the back of the BODY with white thread. Leave a small opening and fill the body with stuffing. Then close up the opening.

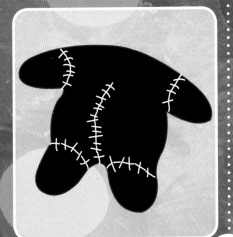

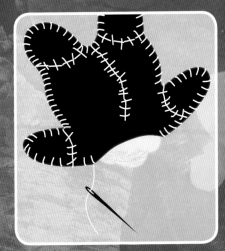

3 Cut the HEAD from black felt. Using white thread, sew a line of 'stitching' to create the mouth and a cross for the left eye.

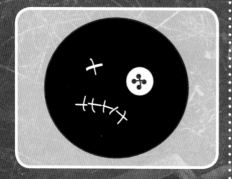

4 Using red thread, sew the button to the HEAD.

VOODOO YOU TRUST?

5 Cut the HEAD BACK from black felt and sew to the back of the HEAD with white thread. Leave a small opening and fill with stuffing. Then close up the opening.

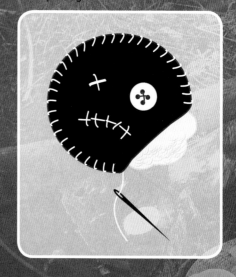

6 Cut the HAT TOP, HAT and HAT BRIM from red felt. Glue the HAT TOP to the top edge of the HAT, then the HAT to the HAT BRIM.

7 Glue the HAT to the top right edge of the HEAD .

9 Using red thread, sew five red dots on to the body. This is done by sewing over the same spot a couple of times.

8 Turn the body over and sew to the HEAD with white thread.

10 Carefully push the five sewing pins into the red spots, taking care not to go through to the back of the zombie and into the table or your finger!

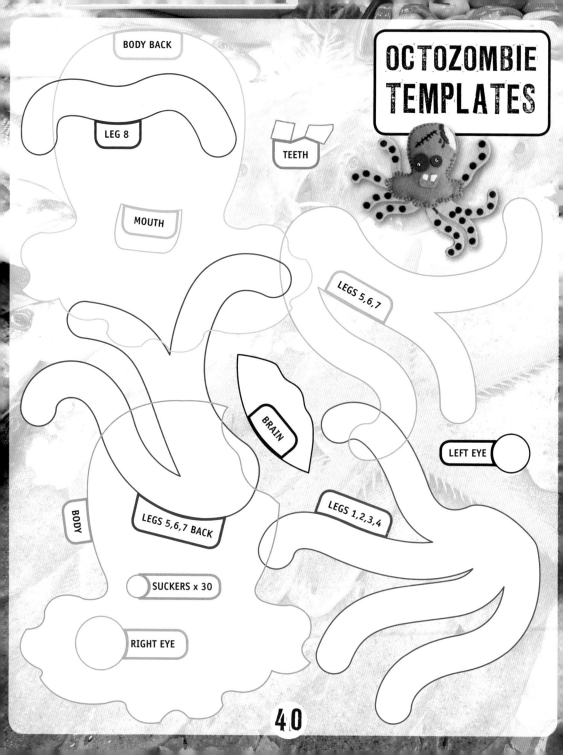

BODY BACK

OCTOZOMBIE TEMPLATES

LEG 8

TEETH

MOUTH

LEGS 5,6,7

BRAIN

LEFT EYE

BODY

LEGS 5,6,7 BACK

LEGS 1,2,3,4

SUCKERS x 30

RIGHT EYE

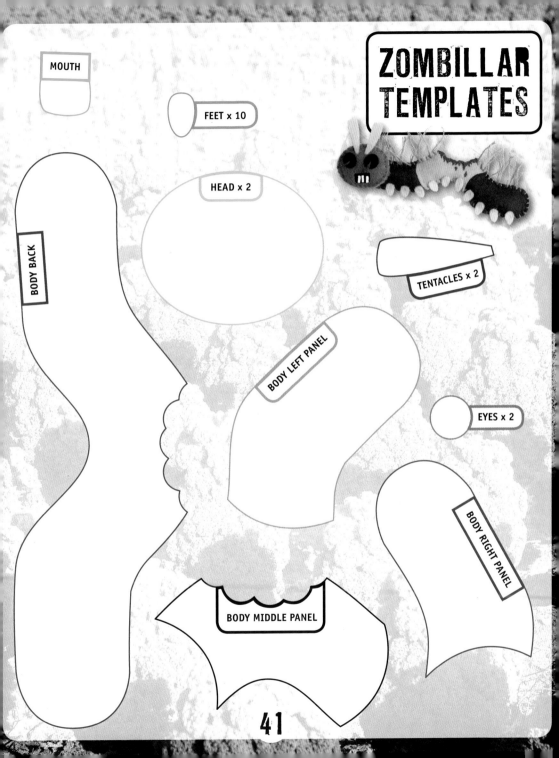

MOUTH

FEET x 10

ZOMBILLAR
TEMPLATES

HEAD x 2

BODY BACK

TENTACLES x 2

BODY LEFT PANEL

EYES x 2

BODY RIGHT PANEL

BODY MIDDLE PANEL

41

ZOMBIE TRAFFIC CONE TEMPLATES

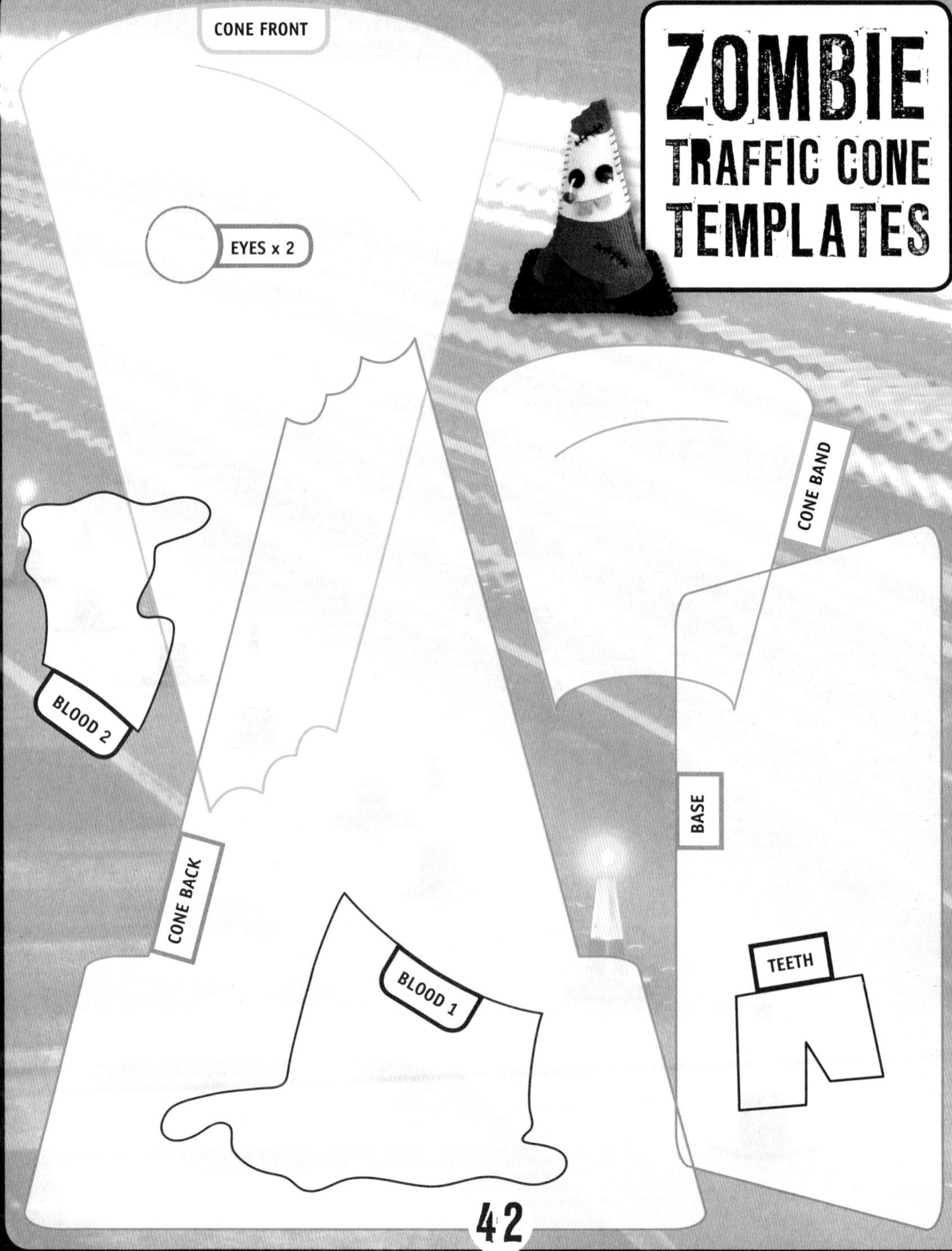
CONE FRONT
EYES x 2
BLOOD 2
CONE BAND
BASE
CONE BACK
BLOOD 1
TEETH

STRAP

RIGHT LEG

LEFT LEG

SCHOOLBOY ZOMBIE TEMPLATES

HEAD x 2

CHEST

EYE

SHORTS

SHIRT

COLLARS x 2

RIGHT ARM

SHIRT POCKET

BODY BACK

LEFT ARM

FLAP

TIE

CAP PEAK

CAP

SATCHEL

43

ZOMBIE PIN BADGE TEMPLATES

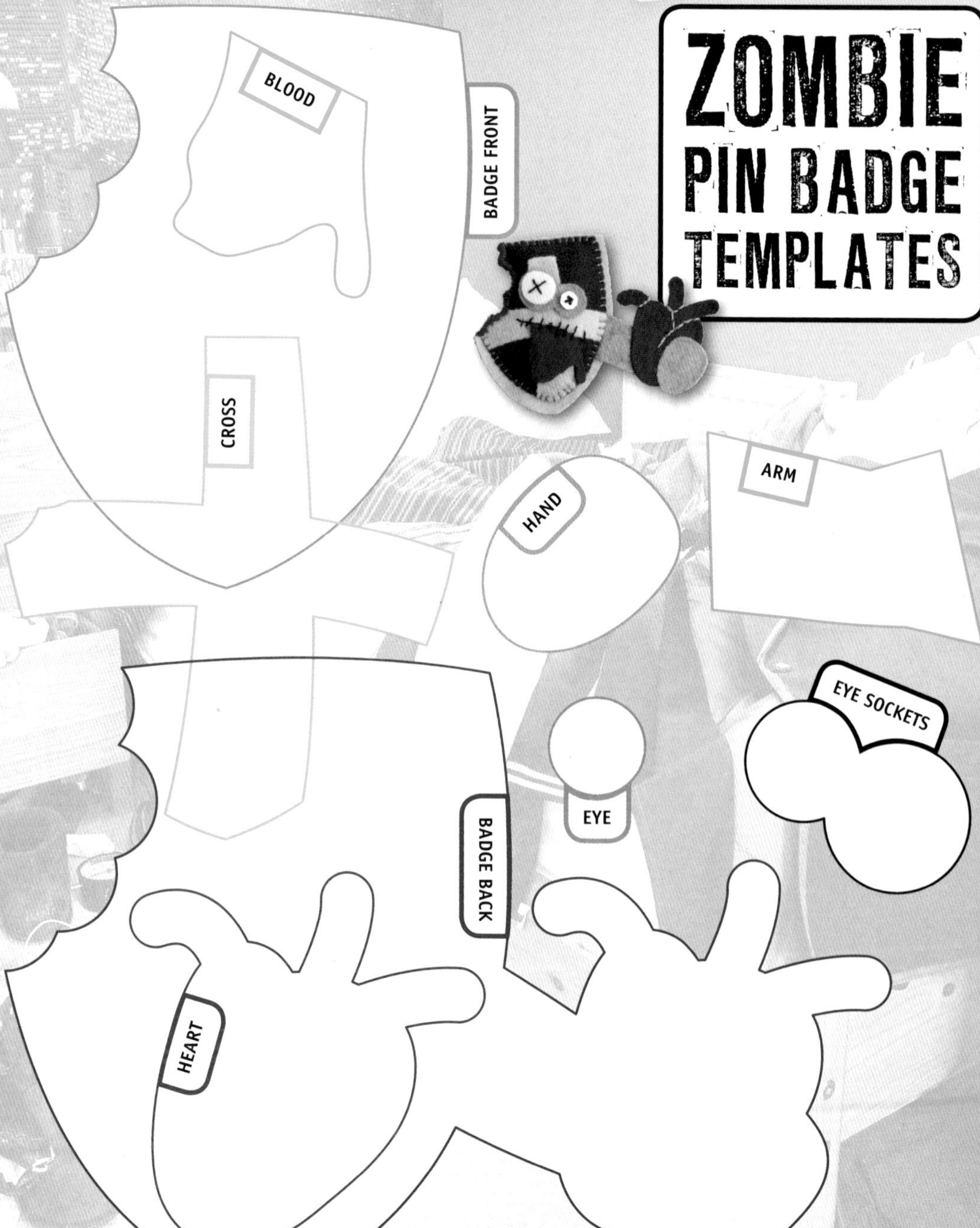

BADGE FRONT

BLOOD

CROSS

HAND

ARM

EYE SOCKETS

EYE

BADGE BACK

HEART

PHONE x 2

TEETH

MOUTH

MOBILE
ZOMPHONE
TEMPLATES

BLOOD

SCREEN

CUT OUT THIS AREA

BUTTONS x 2

EYES x 2

SPEAKER

MICROPHONE

45

VENUS FLY TRAP ZOMBIE TEMPLATES

MOUTH

POT RIM

BACK

LEAF

STEM

POT FRONT

EYES

MOUTH TOP

MOUTH BOTTOM

HEAD

HAT BRIM

VOODOO ZOMBIE TEMPLATES

HEAD BACK

HAT TOP

HAT

BODY

BODY BACK

47